Beeswax crafts

CONTRIBUTORS

Norman Battershill

David Constable

Linda Crouch

Liz Duffin

Polly Pinder

BEESWAX CRAFTS

Candlemaking · Modelling

Beauty creams, soaps and polishes

Encaustic art · Wax crayons

Search Press

First published in Great Britain 1996

Search Press Limited
Wellwood, North Farm Road,
Tunbridge Wells, Kent TN2 3DR

Copyright © Search Press Ltd. 1996

Photographs by Search Press Studios
Photograph on page 6 by Roger Gorringe

Photographs copyright © Search Press Ltd. 1996

ISBN 0 85532 816 9

Suppliers
If you have any difficulty in obtaining any of the
materials and equipment mentioned in this book, then
please write for a current list of stockists, including firms
who operate a mail-order service, to the Publishers.
Search Press Limited, Wellwood,
North Farm Road, Tunbridge Wells,
Kent TN2 3DR, England

Printed in Spain by Elkar S. Coop, Bilbao 48012

A long stemmed rose modelled in beeswax.

Contents

Introduction

Beeswax is a natural product. Worker bees convert honey into wax creating honeycomb patterned combs, and it is these that form the foundation of the beehive. Because of its unique qualities, beeswax has been used for centuries by artists and craftspeople to create beautiful decorative and functional objects.

Thousands of years ago early goldsmiths were casting intricate designs using the lost wax process. Many of the world's greatest bronze figures were created using this method. Excavations into Egyptian tombs have revealed realistic beeswax figures and Madame Tussaud is world famous for her figure gallery and her method of making beeswax heads. For hundreds of years documents, deeds and letters have been sealed with beeswax; often hardening agents and colour were added to make the seals more durable and distinctive.

Candles have been used since the fourth century to light churches during evening services, or to illuminate dark places like the Catacombs, enriching the air with their distinctive, appealing aroma.

The remarkable versatility of beeswax makes it ideal for encaustic art, batik, cosmetics and polish. You can melt it, paint with it, model it or dye it - its creative possibilities are many and varied. We cannot illustrate all the techniques in this book, but we have chosen five crafts as an introduction to beeswax. Whether you own your own beehives, or simply buy the wax from a craft shop, this book will help you to make irresistible items for yourself, or to give as gifts to friends and family.

Opposite
A shallow frame, which has been extended with 'wild' comb by the
bees; it contains capped honey, pollen and capped brood.

Beeswax

Beeswax is available in various sizes, colours and weights. It is formed into chips, solid blocks, and preformed sheets (foundation wax). Chips and blocks come in a range of natural shades; non-toxic wax dyes can be added to melted wax to create a range of colours. Foundation wax sheets measure 30 x 20cm (12 x 8in) and are available in natural shades and about thirty other colours.

Beeswax can be bought from craft shops, beekeepers' suppliers and local beekeepers; if it is bought from the latter it must be reasonably light in colour and filtered to remove any impurities. It has wonderful properties of flexibility, adhesion and viscosity, and is a stable compound. At warm room temperature it is malleable; old beeswax and beeswax at low temperatures can be brittle and fragile. With the exception of the encaustic waxes, which contain light-fast pigments and resins, it will bleach if it is left in bright sunlight.

In this book we show you how to melt, model and mould beeswax to make candles, polish, soaps, cosmetics, encaustic pictures and crayons. The materials and equipment vary for each craft, and these are illustrated and discussed within their respective chapters.

Working with wax

Prepare the work area before starting your project. Cover surfaces and floors with material that can be discarded after you have completed the project. Wear old, comfortable clothes and make sure you have enough room in which to work. Keep liquid wax away from sinks and drains where it could cool and cause a blockage.

To melt wax, you need a double boiler (or a bowl in a shallow pan of water), a heat-resistant jug and a thermometer.

Wax must never be melted in a single pan. To melt the wax safely, use a double boiler, two saucepans (one on top of the other, with water in the bottom one), or a bowl standing in a shallow pan of water. Wax retains its temperature for some time, so be careful when pouring it into moulds or containers. Non-stainless steel, copper or iron will discolour beeswax, so use only aluminium or stainless steel utensils. If it is spilled on carpets or clothing, let it cool, scrape off as much as you can and then iron through absorbent paper to remove the residue. Scrape cold wax off wood surfaces then polish them with a soft cloth. Wash utensils in hot soapy water. White spirit, turpentine or methylated spirit will remove small amounts of cold beeswax.

SAFETY NOTES

Most of the crafts in this book involve the use of molten, liquid beeswax. It is important to be extremely cautious during the melting process. Position container handles over the work surface, and keep children and pets away from the area. Beeswax melts at about 62 to 66°C (143 to 151°F); but you will need to heat it to 82°C (180°F) when pouring it into moulds. At temperatures below 100°C (212°F) it is fairly safe, however, it will start to vaporize at higher temperatures, and it may catch fire. Never use an open flame and never heat beeswax and water together in the same container. If the mixture boils over, spilled water may put out a flame – but the wax may also ignite! Even if small amounts of water are improperly mixed with wax an explosion could occur.

IF THE WAX CATCHES FIRE:

Turn off the heat. Do not move the container. Do not use water to put out the fire. Use a metal lid or damp cloth to smother the flames.

Sheets of foundation wax, smooth sheets made by melting wax on to a template (see pages 21 and 36), a solid beeswax block and wax chips.

Candlemaking

Beeswax candles have a long and luxurious history and evidence of their use dates back to ancient Egypt. For more than three thousand years, beeswax candles were found in only a few places: royal and aristocratic palaces, cathedrals and rich abbeys, and the houses of successful merchants and traders - ordinary people had to make do with dim lamps burning vegetable oil, smoky foul-smelling tapers made from animal tallow, or just the glow of an open fire. Even today, the bright aromatic flame of a well-made beeswax candle casts more than just a glimmer of age-old elegance and mystery.

Opposite
A selection of the different types of beeswax candle that you can make.

Materials and equipment

Apart from the essentials – beeswax and wick – the materials and equipment required for making candles will vary with the type of candle you want to make. You can start with just a craft knife and a chopping board to make candles from sheets of foundation wax, buy a dipping container to make dipped candles, and then add some moulds and mould stands to enlarge your collection. Below and on the page opposite I have illustrated and listed the materials and equipment needed to make all the candles shown in this book.

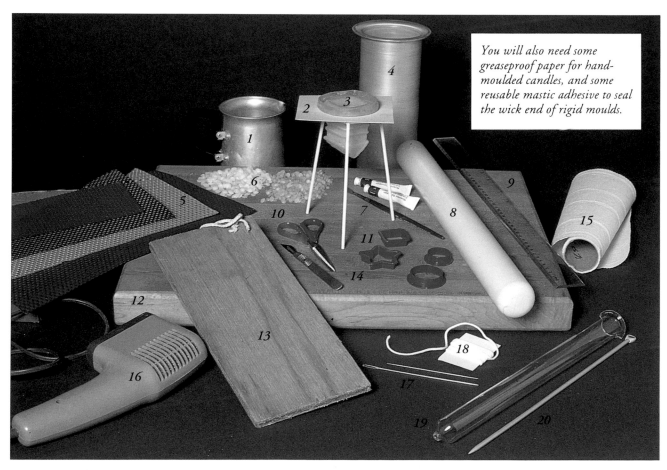

You will also need some greaseproof paper for hand-moulded candles, and some reusable mastic adhesive to seal the wick end of rigid moulds.

1. Heatproof jug.
2. Mould stand and card support.
3. Flexible mould.
4. Dipping cylinder.
5. Foundation wax sheets.
6. Wax chips or beads.
7. Watercolour paints and a brush.
8. Rolling pin.
9. Ruler/straight-edge.
10. Scissors.
11. Pastry cutters.
12. Chopping board.
13. Wooden dipping template.
14. Scalpel/craft knife.
15. Kitchen paper.
16. Hair dryer.
17. Wicking needles.
18. Wicks.
19. Rigid mould.
20. Old knitting needle.

Wick

At the heart of a good candle is the right wick, and this is especially true of beeswax candles. Beeswax is sticky stuff, and does not travel through wick as quickly as other waxes. Slow delivery of wax means an inefficient flame, which makes for a bad candle – therefore you must use a wick that is thicker than that you would for a same size of paraffin wax candle.

Beeswax wick is round, not flat like that used in paraffin wax candles. Round wick is manufactured in a range of sizes, which different makers grade according to different systems.

The wick has a weave structure which makes them burn best in one direction – so it has a top and bottom – this is illustrated in the enlargement (right). Usually they are supplied in rolls or hanks with the top of the wick as the loose end. It is a good idea to tie a small knot in the top end of loose lengths of wick.

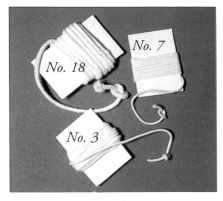

Wick is sized for different diameters of candle:

No. 18 – for 50–55mm (2–2¹/₄in) diameter candles.

No. 7 – for 15–18mm (about ⁵/₈in) diameter candles.

No. 3 – for 8–10mm (about ³/₈in) diameter candles.

Using foundation sheets

Foundation-sheet candles are simple to make, and add a touch of class to any dinner table. A sheet of wax will make a candle 300mm (12in) high and 20mm (³/₄in) in diameter. Roll candles on a moist kitchen surface or chopping board and use a craft knife and straight-edge to cut them to size. Beeswax is best worked at a warm room temperature. If beeswax sheets have been stored in a cool place, they can be warmed slightly with a hair-dryer – but do not overheat.

Column candle

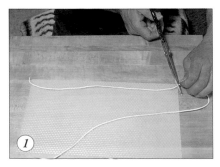

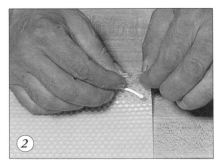

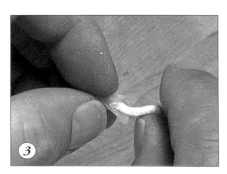

1. Cut a wick about 15mm (⁵/₈in) longer than the length of the sheet.

2. Pinch a fingernail of wax from the bottom corner of the sheet.

3. Squeeze it around and into the top of the wick.

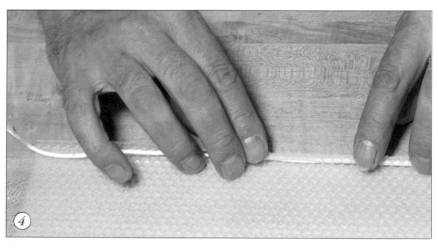

4. Lay the wick along the edge of the sheet, with the waxed end just protruding from one end. Working on one area at a time, carefully turn the edge of the sheet over the wick.

5. Roll the sheet smoothly, keeping the ends square.

6. If necessary, trim the bottom of the candle with a craft knife so that it sits squarely.

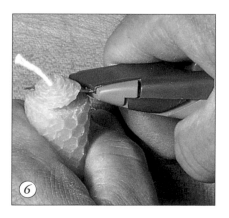

Spiral candles

Cut a sheet of wax diagonally into triangles, and then use the rolling method on pages 13 and 14 to make two spiral candles.

Two-tone spiral candles

1. By using two triangles of contrasting colours, you can make a more spectacular candle. Trim 10mm (³⁄₈in) from the base of one triangle, then align the two triangles by their bases and vertical edges, with the smaller triangle below the larger one.

2. Take extra care when folding the double thickness of sheet over the wick, and then roll up the wax to form the spiral.

Column and spiral candles made from sheets of foundation wax.

These foundation-wax lanterns make a fun addition to a party buffet.

Lanterns

Foundation wax can be cut and shaped to make many other simple candles. These lanterns are easy to make. For each lantern you need a 200 x 75mm (8 x 3in) sheet of yellow wax, a 140 x 100mm ($5\frac{1}{2}$ x 4in) sheet of red wax, and 100mm (4in) of No. 7 wick. Use the method described on pages 14–15 to roll a 75mm (3in) yellow candle.

1. Using a craft knife and a straight-edge, make a series of cuts, about 6mm ($\frac{1}{4}$in) apart, across the sheet of red wax.

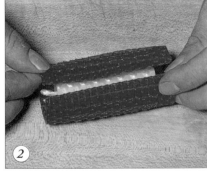

2. Gently roll the red wax around the yellow candle and carefully seal the overlap to form a tube slightly larger than the yellow candle.

3. Squeeze the bottom of the tube around the base of the candle. Now, carefully push the top of the tube downwards so that the slats start to open up. Use your fingers and the handle of your craft knife to adjust the shape of the slats.

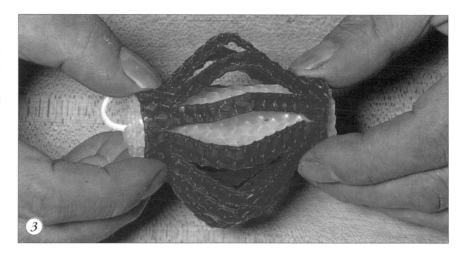

Floating water lilies

Here is another simple exercise using foundation wax – a floating water lily candle. For each lily, you will need four 5cm (2in) circles of green wax, a 20 x 100mm ($^3/_4$in x 4in) strip of yellow wax and a 30mm ($1^1/_4$in) length of No. 7 wick.

1. Press the four circles together to make the lily pad, and then dish out the leaves slightly with your fingers and thumbs. Do not leave any gaps.

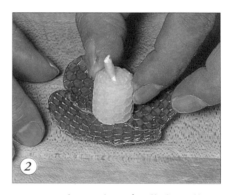

2. Wax the wick and roll the yellow strip to form a short cylindrical candle as described on pages 13–14. Place the candle in the lily pad.

3. Place the candle in a glass of water to ensure that it floats without filling up with water – adjust the shape of the leaves if necessary.

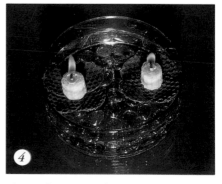

4. Make a second water lily and place them in a decorative bowl filled with water. When lit they make an exciting table centre-piece.

Dipping

Dipping is the traditional method of making beeswax candles; you have to build up a candle, layer by layer, until it is the required size.

You will need a container of hot wax (heated to about 82°C (180°F), some wick and a place to hang the candles between dips.

The ideal container is a purpose-made dipping-can standing in a large pan of hot water, but you can use any tall metal or heatproof glass container. The size of container is important – you cannot make a candle taller than the depth of wax in your container. Also, with narrow containers the level can drop quite rapidly as dipping proceeds, especially if you are making more than one candle at a time, and you will probably need to top up the level with hot wax regularly.

Column candles

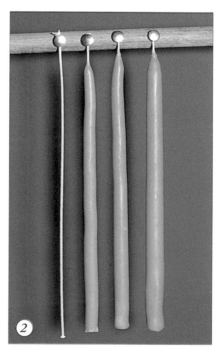

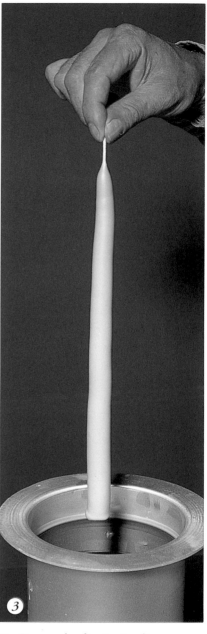

1. Cut a No. 7 wick allowing an extra length at the top for hanging the candle between dips. Soak the wick in hot wax for about one minute. Pull it out of the container, let it cool slightly and then draw it through your fingers to straighten and remove all excess wax.

2. Use a drawing pin to hang it up to cool. Now dip the waxed wick into the container for one or two seconds, pull it out and hang it up again for about thirty to fifty seconds. If you watch the wax, you will note how it changes colour and opacity as it cools.

3. Repeat the dipping/cooling process until you have a candle of the desired thickness. If a candle develops a wrinkled surface, you are not waiting long enough between dips. The wax beneath the outer skin is still 'liquid', and is moving during dipping and forming the wrinkles.

Spiral candles

While your dipped candle is still warm it will be malleable enough to model into other shapes. Here I show you how to make a spiral candle. Try other shapes – if you do not like the result, you can melt the wax and start again.

1. Using a dampened rolling pin on a dampened surface, roll a candle flat, working it down to about 6mm (¹/₄in) thick.

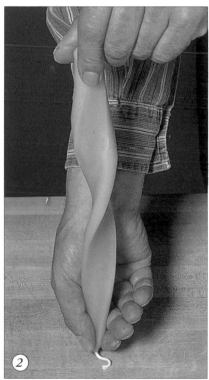

2. Now, twist the candle into an spiral by turning your hand as you draw your fingers along the flattened surface.

Dipping is the traditional method of making beeswax candles.

Using templates

For additional variation, try making your own sheets of wax by dipping a dampened template into melted wax. Properly cut and smoothed 6mm ($^1/_4$in) thick glass makes the best wax template, but good quality plywood of the same thickness can also be used.

Templates can be made in a variety of shapes . Allow enough room for holding the template during dipping, and attach a string loop for hanging it up.

1. Thoroughly soak the template in water, wipe off the excess water and then dip it into melted wax for one or two seconds. Hang up to cool in the same way as ordinary dipped candles. Continue dipping and cooling until you have the required thickness. You will need between five and eight dips to get a sheet of reasonable thickness.

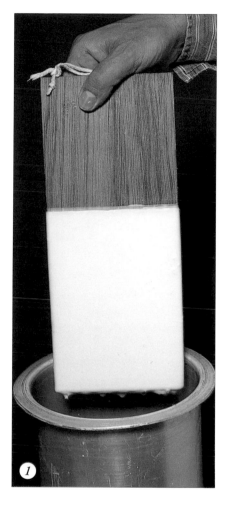

2. When the last dipped layer has gone translucent, cut around the template with a craft knife.

3. Peel off a sheet of wax from each side, and then roll them up with a waxed wick as shown on pages 13–15.

If you cut a rectangular sheet into two triangles, you can roll and then shape the spiral edges into beautiful flaring shapes. Use a hair-dryer to maintain the temperature of the wax while working on these edges.

Additional interest can be created by dipping a few layers in one shade of wax, and then dipping a few more layers in a contrasting shade.

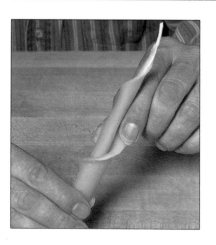

Opposite
A selection of candles made from dipped templates.

Hand-modelled candles

You can also model with cooled wax to make ball candles, mushrooms, and other different shapes.

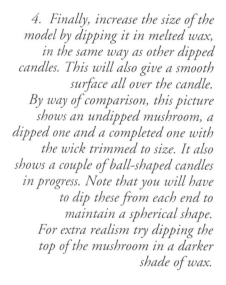

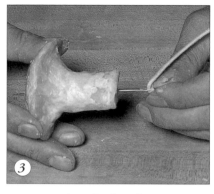

1. Place a sheet of greaseproof paper in a bowl and pour in some melted wax. Let it cool for about half an hour and then remove it from the paper. Although set, it will still be soft enough to mould in your hand.

2. Mould it into shape; here I am making a mushroom-shaped candle. At this stage, do not worry too much about the surface finish – all you want to get is a rough form of a mushroom.

3. Wax a length of wick in melted wax, thread a large-holed wicking needle and then pass the wick through the candle.

4. Finally, increase the size of the model by dipping it in melted wax, in the same way as other dipped candles. This will also give a smooth surface all over the candle. By way of comparison, this picture shows an undipped mushroom, a dipped one and a completed one with the wick trimmed to size. It also shows a couple of ball-shaped candles in progress. Note that you will have to dip these from each end to maintain a spherical shape. For extra realism try dipping the top of the mushroom in a darker shade of wax.

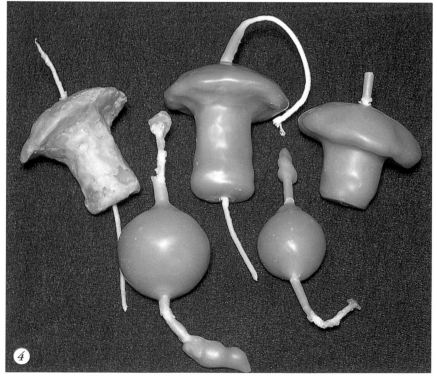

Moulded candles

There are lots of different candle moulds that you can buy – some are rigid, some are flexible. You will need a mould stand and, for the smaller diameter moulds, some scrap card to support the mould in the stand. You can improvise and, say, use a yoghurt pot as a mould, but you will only end up with a yoghurt-pot candle. Because beeswax is a relatively precious commodity, it is worth investing in a purpose-made, candle mould to give a more attractive shape.

> To decide how much wax to melt, fill a mould with water and measure its contents. For every 10g or 10cc (10 fluid oz) of water, you need 9gm (9oz) of wax. Dry the mould thoroughly afterwards.

Rigid moulds

Rigid moulds are available in glass or plastic. Plastic ones do allow you to enlarge the wick hole to accommodate the thicker wicks required for beeswax candles. However, here I am using a glass mould which was made for beeswax candle wicks.

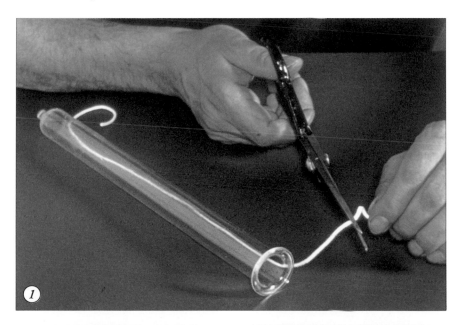

1. First, cut a length of wick 75mm (3in) longer than the mould and wax it as shown on page 18.

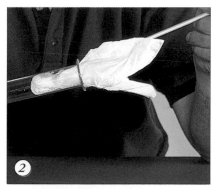

2. Now prepare the mould for use. Pour some liquid soap in the mould and then use a knitting needle and a piece of tissue to spread it around.

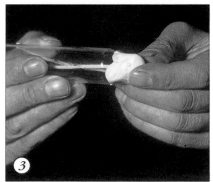

3. Thread the waxed wick through the top of the mould and seal the end with re-usable mastic adhesive. You can buy proper mould sealants, but mastic adhesive works just as well.

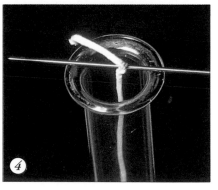

4. Invert the mould, gently pull the wick so that it lies in the middle of the mould and then hold in place with a wicking needle.

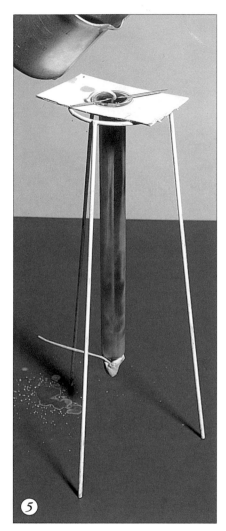

5

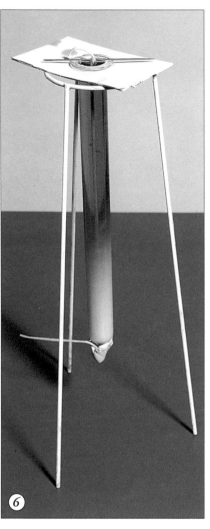

6

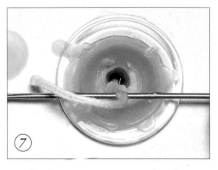

⑦

7. As the wax starts to cool a skin forms over the open end. Below this skin the wax continues to cool, and to shrink, forming a cavity just below the surface. Break the skin with a wicking needle and top up the resulting cavity with hot wax. Do not over-fill, otherwise the candle may be difficult to extract.

  If you do not break the skin and top up the mould with wax, you will find that when you burn the candle, a large and unsightly hole is revealed at the centre.

5. Make a cardboard support for the neck of the mould and place the inverted mould in a stand. Heat the wax then pour it slowly into the mould.

6. The wax in the mould will initially cloud, then clear. Wait two minutes, then tap the sides of the mould to release any air bubbles that may spoil the surface of the finished candle. Gradually you will see the wax beginning to set from the bottom upwards.

8

8. When completely cool, remove the sealant from the top of the mould, invert the mould, and gently shake the candle free.

A selection of moulded candles made with rigid moulds (left) and flexible moulds (right).

Flexible moulds

Beeswax can also be cast in flexible rubber or plastic moulds to make fruits, flowers and other fun candles. These moulds must be well supported. Here I am using a mould stand, but you can use a piece of card mounted over a jar or jug. Melt a quantity of wax and prepare a waxed wick as shown on page 18.

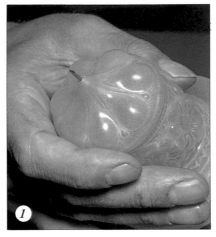

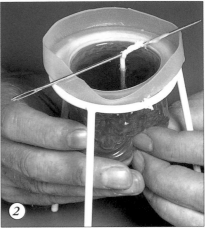

1. New flexible moulds do not have a top opening for the wick, so you must make one by piercing the mould with a wicking needle. Thread the wick and support it centrally within the mould with a wicking needle.

2. Place the mould on its stand and pour in the wax. While the wax is still in a molten state gently squeeze the mould to release trapped air.

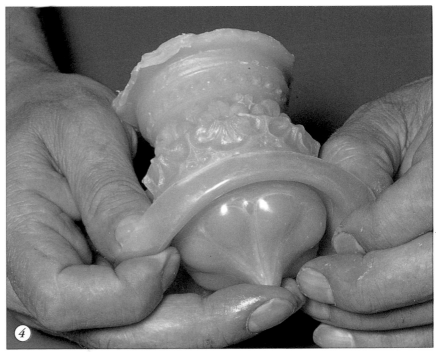

3. When a skin has formed over the top of the mould, break it with a wicking needle and top up the cavity with more molten wax.

4. When the candle has completely cooled, smear the outside of the mould with liquid soap and carefully ease the mould off the candle by peeling it back all round.

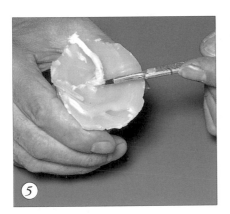

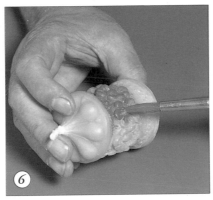

You can smooth and flatten the bottom of the candle by placing it on a hot flat surface (the bottom of your melting pan or a piece of aluminium foil placed on the sole of a hot iron).

5. Cut of the excess wick at the base of the candle with a craft knife.

6. You can now decorate the candle with watercolour paint if required.

Beehive candles in different shapes and sizes made using flexible moulds.

Modelling

Modelling

Beeswax is one of the oldest modelling materials known to man. It is still used by sculptors for preliminary models and by foundries in the lost wax method of casting. Here I have used it in a more modern way to make flowers and small models.

Sheets of wax are pliable when worked in a warm room with warm fingers, and will stick together when pressed firmly. The simplest flowers are made from sheets of foundation wax which are available in a vast rainbow of colours. However, for really delicate and more realistic flowers you will need to make your own smooth sheets of wax.

You can also cast beeswax in moulds, in much the same way as for candles, and mould cooled wax by hand (it remains malleable for some time) to make lots of other types of models.

Beeswax is classed as a hard wax (its melting point is 63°C, 145°F). Although pieces can be 'welded' together by the heat from your fingers, when cooled the wax is hard enough to be washed in warm (not hot) soapy water.

Opposite
BUNCH OF GRAPES
Half grapes were made in a ball-shaped ice mould, wired together in pairs and then overdipped in liquid wax. The individual grapes were then wired into a bunch and the stems painted with liquid wax.

Materials

Beeswax flowers are made in the same way as other artificial flowers, and the materials used are readily available from florists and cake-decorating shops. Apart from the melting equipment and the beeswax which are described on page 8, you will need the materials shown here.

You will also find some of these items useful, particularly the stub wires, when making other types of wax models.

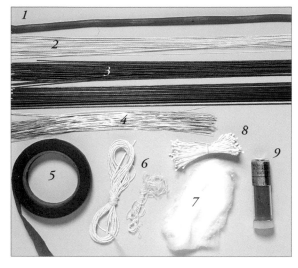

1. Covered mains cable.
2. No. 26 or 28 gauge coloured covered wires.
3. Florists stub wires.
4. Fine florist wires.
5. Stem binding tape (available in various colours).
6. Cotton threads of different thicknesses for stamens.
7. Cotton wool.
8. Ready-made stamens.
9. Petal dusting colour.

Foundation wax flowers

Foundation wax is very easy to work with; it comes in a variety of colours and can be used to make some wonderful wax flowers. I have included a pattern and instructions for making a poinsettia, and I also show other examples.

Poinsettia

In addition to the materials mentioned above, you will need one sheet each of red and green foundation wax and some thin card for making the templates.

Trace these patterns on to thin card. The diagrams are full size and the quantities shown are for one flower stem. To make the complete plant you will need three stems.

Green calix – cut one.

Red petals – cut three small, four medium and six large.

Green leaves – cut one large and three small.

Red flower centre – cut three.

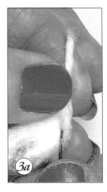

1. Use a craft knife to cut intricate shapes

2. Use a pair of scissors to cut rounded shapes.

3. Twist a wisp of cotton wool around the top 20mm (³/₄in) of 180mm (6in) stub wire, fold over the top half and bind the stem tightly with stem binding tape.

4. Melt off-cuts of red and green wax; I find a poaching pan most suitable for small pieces of wax.

5. Dip the cotton wool tip of the stem into the red wax.

6. Cut lengths of white and green-covered wire for each petal and leaf. Gently press each wire on to the wax shapes and then paint over each wire with red or green liquid wax to hold them in place.

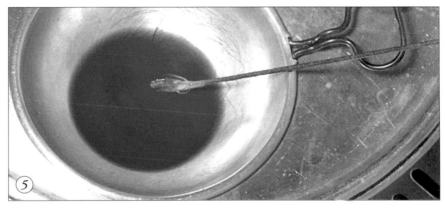

7. Take five
ready-made,
double-ended
stamens, fold
them in half
and press on to
waxed tip of the
stem.

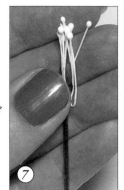

8. Now, start to assemble the petals.
First, press three small pieces of wax
around the stamens to form the
centre of the flower.

9. Bend the petal wires as shown
and then press each petal into place
around the centre. Start with the
three small ones, then add the four
medium ones and finally press on the
six large ones.

10. Attach the calyx, pressing it
firmly on to the base of the petals and
the stem.

11. Gently curve and shape the petals until they look natural.

12. Bind the stem with tape, starting at the calyx, and add one pair of small leaves approximately 30mm (1¹/₄in) below the calyx. Continue taping the stem adding the third small leaf a further 30mm (1¹/₄in) down the stem.

13. Make three flower stems and then join them together with more tape adding the three large leaves in a rosette below the small leaves.

33

14. *The finished plant can be pushed into a plant pot filled with a block of polystyrene or dry oasis. Cover the top with peat or gravel.*

WATER LILY PAD

The petals for this foundation-wax water lily are not wired, they are pressed on to a 30mm (1¼in) diameter disc starting from the outside and working in towards the centre.

The centre of the flower is a cone of yellow wax surrounded by stamens made from cotton thread dipped in yellow wax.

The lily pad is cut from a sheet of green foundation. The stem is green foundation wrapped around a piece of string and pressed into place.

ORCHID

The orchid is made with wired petals on a cotton-wool-tipped stem. The centre was moulded from off-cuts of wax and the petals were shaded with red petal dust brushed on with a soft brush.

Hand-made wax sheets

The flowers in this section are made from thin sheets of wax coloured with candle dyes. Blocks of candle dye, which are very strongly coloured wax, can be used to colour the wax. Mix them with the melted wax as you would paints to get the desired colour. If you are using yellow wax, to make a good green, for example, you may need to add a little blue and brown dye.

You will need a piece of plywood, about 150 x 200mm (6 x 8in) in size. The surface must be well sanded and not have any wax, paint, etc., on it. Saturate the plywood in a bowl of cold water.

> Sometimes, you will need thicker sheets of wax. These can be made by pouring more layers of wax over the first.

1. Melt a quantity of beeswax in a bowl in a shallow pan of water. Add the dye and stir well.

2. Remove the plywood from the bowl of cold water and mop off excess water with a tea towel or a piece of kitchen roll. Ladle the molten wax down the board, letting the excess wax run back into the bowl of wax.

3. Immediately pour some cold water over the wax to cool it.

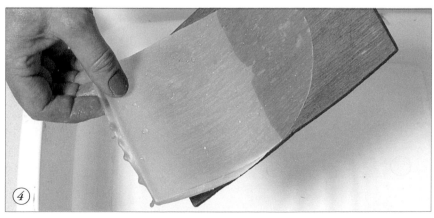

4. Carefully lift the wax sheet off the board.

A bowl of irises

A bowl of Iris Reticulata could brighten up a dark corner in the spring. These irises are the purple variety, but you could use a paler mauve or yellow. When using blue or purple dyes you need a very pale beeswax to give a good clean colour.

Trace the patterns on to thin card. The diagram is full size and the quantities shown are for one flower stem. To make the complete plant you will need three stems. The full arrangement also includes three sets of bud stems which do not require petals B and C.

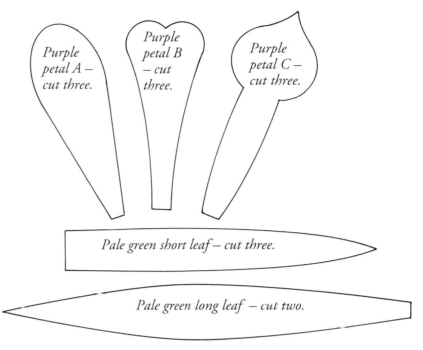

Purple petal A – cut three.

Purple petal B – cut three.

Purple petal C – cut three.

Pale green short leaf – cut three.

Pale green long leaf – cut two.

1. Using a craft knife or a pair of scissors, cut out the petals and leaves. This set is for one open flower stem.

2. Curve and shape petals A in your fingers. Rub the edges to soften the wax and create a thin sharp outline.

A shaped leaf beside the original flat one.

 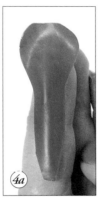 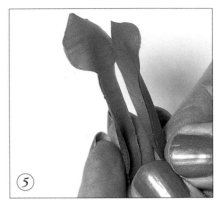

3.   Make a 90mm (3¹/₂in) cotton wool-tipped, stub wire stem (see page 31) and press the petals around the stem so that they overlap each other.

4.   Shape the petal shapes B (4a) and C (4b), curving them as shown.

5.   Join one petal B on to one petal C to form a tube with the narrow parts of the petals. The wider parts of the petals curve away from each other.

6.   Press the base of the tube on to the stem. Repeat with the remaining two pairs of petals, pressing them together and smoothing them on to the stem.

7.   Soften and shape the two long leaves and place around the stem with their points coming up between the petals.

8.   Shape the three short leaves and attach them around the stem in a fan shape to complete one stem. Make two more open flower stems.

9.   Make three bud stems in a similar way but using just two petal shapes A. Wrap these around the stem tightly as shown and then add leaves as for the full flower.

10.   (Opposite) Push the flowers and buds into a block of dry oasis fixed in a bowl or basket. Cover the surface with decorative gravel to simulate a scree garden.

(10)

STRELITZIAS

This arrangement is made from hand-made sheets of coloured wax. The stems of these flowers are much thicker and I used plastic-coated mains electrical cable. Each leaf is made from two sheets of wax, sandwiched together around stub wire covered in stem binding tape. The pieces should be pressed together well and the veins marked with a knitting needle or an empty ball-point pen.

Opposite

BOWL OF ROSES

Hand-made wax sheets are also used for these roses. The side leaves are attached to fine wires that are twisted around the stem below the top leaf. The veins are marked with a knitting needle and the edges of the leaves are serrated by snipping them with a pair of scissors. For strength the base of each leaf is painted with a little molten wax.

Modelling

Making other wax models

The simplest form of model is one made in a commercially produced mould (see moulded candles on pages 23–27). Beeswax can be difficult to remove from rubber moulds, but a smear of glycerine rubbed all over the inside of the mould will help. Silicone rubber moulds are much more effective and do not require a release agent.

GOOSE

The goose was made in a polyurethane mould and then attached to a base moulded in a shallow plastic container. The eyes are small balls of brown wax pressed into place.

SNOWMAN

I melted bleached beeswax and allowed it to cool. When the wax began to set, I whipped it with a fork, scraping the set wax from the sides, and mixing it until it formed the texture of stiff meringue. When it was cool enough to handle, I shaped a large ball for the snowman's body. I then formed a smaller ball for the head and attached this to the body using a cocktail stick for stability. I made the features from small scraps of wax. I used a sheet of wax for the scarf. I made the hat by dipping a piece of wet 25mm (1in) wooden dowel several times into molten wax. I then attached a brim made from a thin sheet.

OWL

This was cast in a silicone rubber mould. The eyes were painted with a dark wood stain.

Opposite

WISHING WELL

The model opposite is made from natural undyed beeswax. using a number of techniques. The 'bricks' were made in an ice-cube tray and cemented together using molten wax. The thick sheets for the sides and roof were made by floating molten beeswax on to the surface of hot boiled water in a large flat pan and leaving it to set. The resulting sheets were carefully cut into shape with a warm knife. The leaves and flowers were attached to No. 26 gauge white-covered wire. The winding and bucket handles were made of string soaked in beeswax. The bucket and the tiles were made from thin hand-made sheets of wax.

Beauty creams, soaps and polishes

Beeswax has been used as a cosmetic ingredient for hundreds of years. In its natural state it does not cause allergic reactions when applied to the skin. Because of its unique qualities it is still widely used in the manufacture of solid fragrances, facial and hand creams, skin softeners, lotions, ointments, eye shadow and lipstick. Here are recipes for five creams and a soap which can easily be made at home. All the ingredients are natural. However, those with particularly sensitive skins should be cautious as even the mildest ingredients can sometimes cause a reaction.

Beeswax is also very good as the base ingredient for furniture and other types of polish. Polishes are made in much the same way as the cosmetics so I have included a few recipes which I hope you will find of interest.

Opposite
A selection of creams and soaps that you can make.

General ingredients

The ingredients for creams, soap and polishes can be bought at most
chemists, health stores and DIY shops. There are also good mail order
companies who deal specifically with essential oils, waxes and herbs.
The illustration below is by no means complete but it does give you
an indication of the different types of ingredients that you can use.

Beauty creams:
1. *Rose and orange-flower water.*
2. *Borax.*
3. *Liquid paraffin*
4. *Glycerin*
5. *Coconut oil.*
6. *Cocoa butter*
7. *Food colouring.*
8. *Essential oils (various)*
9. *White and yellow beeswax .*
10. *Vegetable, nut and mineral oils.*
11. *Lanolin.*
12. *Comphrey leaves (dried).*

Soap:
13. *Tallow.*
14. *Honey.*
15. *Caustic soda.*
You will also need some of the
ingredients used for creams.

Polishes:
16. *Liquid soap and soap flakes.*
17. *White spirit.*
18. *Pine oil*
19. *Turpentine.*
20. *Linseed oil.*
21. *Neatsfoot oil.*
22. *Carnuba wax.*
23. *Methylated spirit (for cleaning*
surfaces before polishing).

Beauty creams

I have included five recipes for different types of cream (see pages 50–51). There is a huge variety of perfumes that you can add to these creams; I have suggested some, but if you have a particular favourite, use it instead.

> The easiest way to melt ingredients is in screw-topped jars - small clean preserve jars are ideal. Label the lids. Remove the lids while the jars are being heated, but do not forget which is which when replacing the lids after the contents have cooled.

Melting and mixing ingredients

The method of melting and mixing the ingredients is common to all of the creams, and is shown here; there are slight variations with some creams and I have noted these with the individual recipes.

1. Place broken pieces of solid ingredients (wax, coconut oil, cocoa butter) in separate jars and heat them in a pan of water, simmering until they have melted.

2. Measure the melted ingredients into a heat resistant basin over a pan of simmering water.

3. Measure and stir in the oils (glycerin, liquid paraffin), but not the perfumed essential oil.

4. Pour the water (rose water, orange-flower water) into a heat resistant jug. Add the borax and heat gently until it dissolves.

5. Remove the basin (melted wax and oils) from the pan and add the borax water.

6. Mix thoroughly. Place the basin in a shallow dish of cold water and continue beating.

7. Add the essential oil and beat until the mixture cools and thickens.

These creams should last for many years. I recently discovered a couple of jars at the back of a cupboard – both made in 1978 and both perfectly usable. Some people do recommend that creams, particularly those containing herbal waters, be stored in the fridge, but one of the creams I found was made with elderflower water!

8. Transfer the cream to pretty screw-topped jars. When the cream is completely cold cover with a disc of waxed paper or kitchen foil then secure the lid tightly. Attach a label with the name of the cream and the date.

Recipes for creams

Chapped hand treatment

5 tablespoons yellow beeswax
3 tablespoons coconut oil

This is a firm cream which acts as a wonderful balm when gently applied to rough, chapped hands. It is also an excellent barrier if your hands are to be immersed in water for long periods.

Follow stages 1, 2, 6 and 8 of the general method. The cream will set fairly solid when cold. Use a small wooden spatula to transfer it from the jar to your hands. As soon as application starts it will melt into the skin.

Daily hand cream

2 tablespoons white beeswax
3 teaspoons cocoa butter
3 teaspoons anhydrous lanolin
2 tablespoons liquid paraffin
2 teaspoons glycerin
2 teaspoons almond oil
2 tablespoons orange-flower water
$1/4$ teaspoon borax
$1/2$ teaspoon essential sandalwood oil

This cream makes the hands beautifully soft, especially the finger tips which sometimes become irritatingly dry. A slight oily residue will be left after the initial application; if you can bear this it will help the dryness and will soon be absorbed.

Follow all stages of the general method. The lanolin, which is semi-solid, can be measured straight into the basin without first melting. The sandalwood oil is optional, it helps to soften the skin and also has a lovely smell. Do make sure that you buy a pure essential oil rather than a synthetic one.

Rose cleansing cream

2 tablespoons white beeswax
1 tablespoon emulsifying wax
4 tablespoons unperfumed baby (mineral) oil
3 tablespoons rose-water
$1/4$ teaspoon borax
5 drops essential rose oil
3 drops red food colour

A cream similar to this was developed two thousand years ago by the Greeks. Apply it to the face and throat. Leave it for a few minutes, then gently remove it with cotton wool soaked in an equal mixture of witch-hazel and rose-water or, for those with very dry skin, three parts rose-water to one part witch-hazel.

Follow all stages of the general method. Baby oil is used for this cream because it is not absorbed by the skin. Essential rose oil is very expensive; if you feel it is too extravagant substitute it with essential rose geranium oil. The red food colour is harmless, it will not turn you pink, it simply gives the cream a pretty hue.

Rich moisturising cream

$1^1/_2$ tablespoons white beeswax
1 tablespoon emulsifying wax
2 tablespoons anhydrous lanolin
5 teaspoons avocado oil
1 teaspoon glycerin
3 vitamin E capsules
5 tablespoons water
3 tablespoons rose-water
$^1/_4$ teaspoon borax
6 drops essential lavender oil

Used to replace lost skin moisture, this recipe produces a light rich cream which can be applied to the face before taking a bath – steam will help the skin to absorb the oils and water.

Follow all stages of the general method. The semi-solid lanolin can be measured straight into the basin without first melting. Pierce the vitamin E capsules over the basin so that the oil drops straight into the mixture.

Comfrey nourishing cream

2 tablespoons yellow beeswax
2 tablespoons cocoa butter
3 tablespoons sesame oil
1 tablespoon wheatgerm oil
2 tablespoons dried comfrey leaves
5 tablespoons boiling water
$^1/_4$ teaspoon borax
5 drops essential lime oil

An infusion of comfrey and the sweet scent of limes make this a special cream. Both the leaves and roots of comfrey contain allantoin, a protein which promotes cell renewal. Apply the cream to the hands, face and neck just before going to bed.

Before starting the cream, make the comfrey infusion. Place the dried leaves in a small basin, stir in the boiling water then cover them with a porous cloth or paper towel. Leave them for two to three hours then strain them through doubled muslin or two paper towels. Add the borax to the water then follow all stages of the general method.

Soap

I have included just one recipe for soap which is perfumed by adding citronella and lemon oils. The scent is initially very strong but during the soap's maturing period it becomes much less powerful. Other essential oils, which have a lovely fragrance and are suitable for soap making, are ylang ylang and lavender. Be sure to use only pure essential oils; synthetic oils do not contain beneficial properties and may be harmful to the skin.

The ingredients are available from chemists, herb stores or specialist mail order companies. Tallow (clarified animal fat) is difficult to buy but is very easy and cheaper to make (see instructions below).

You will need about six plastic moulds (yoghurt pots and small margarine tubs are ideal) but make sure that they taper outwards to make removal of the soap easier. Small pressed flowers or leaves can be placed in the bottom of the mould before adding the soap.

> Caustic soda (sodium hydroxide) is an essential ingredient of soap. It seems very odd that such a severe substance eventually produces a mild and gentle bar of soap, but it does!
>
> Caustic soda must be handled with care – wear rubber gloves and a plastic apron. Do not stand directly over the jug of caustic solution.

Making tallow

Tallow is hard fat from ruminating animals that has been separated from membranes, etc., by melting and clarifying. It is very easy to make at home. Ask your local butcher for 1kg (2lb) of minced beef fat, which he may offer to give you, and clarify it as follows.

1. Put five tablespoons of water and one of salt in a heavy pan. Add the minced fat, simmer until it has melted then turn off the heat and allow it to cool for about ten minutes.

2. Carefully strain the melted fat twice through double muslin, or two paper towels, into a large screw-topped glass jar (an old, clean coffee jar is ideal).
Before the fat sets pour 200ml (7 fl oz) into one of the jugs. The remainder will last indefinitely, and can be kept until you want to make another batch of soap.

Honey soap

200ml (7 fl oz) tallow
1¹/₂ tablespoons yellow beeswax
2 tablespoons coconut oil
1 tablespoon cocoa butter
1 tablespoon wheatgerm oil
¹/₂ teaspoon citronella
6 drops essential lemon oil
1 tablespoon clear honey
150ml (5 fl oz) cold water
2 tablespoons caustic soda

This recipe makes a lovely satin soap which produces a good lather and does not leave the skin feeling dry or taut.

Melt the wax, coconut oil and cocoa butter separately (see stage 1 on page 47) then measure them into the jug of tallow. Stir in the citronella, lemon oil, wheatgerm oil and honey.

1. Pour the water into another jug, carefully add the caustic soda and stir until dissolved. A chemical reaction takes place and the solution will heat up of its own accord. Leave to cool for five minutes – place your hand underneath the jug to ascertain the temperature.

2. Slowly pour the soda solution into the jug of oils mixing continuously; the mixture will thicken quite quickly, so . . .

3. . . . pour it immediately into the moulds.

4. Leave the soap to set for two days then carefully remove it from the moulds and place on a paper towel to mature for about two weeks.

Polishes

Throughout history beeswax has been used as the main ingredient of all sorts of polish. There are two basic types of polish that you can make. Paste polishes are a simple blend of wax and a solvent – traditionalists will use pure turpentine, but white spirit and other solvents are equally suitable. Emulsion polish (furniture cream), is a mixture of two liquids which do not normally mix: wax (and a solvent) and water (in the form of a soap solution). Here I give a few recipes for you to try. In each of the following recipes melt the wax, warm up the other ingredients, mix thoroughly and pour the polish into tins or wide-mouthed, screw-topped jars.

> Do try experimenting with these recipes – you can add essential oils, and you can alter the consistency by varying the amount of solvent.

Basic paste polish

250g (10oz) beeswax
500ml (1pint) solvent (turpentine or white spirit)

This simple blend of wax and a solvent makes an easy-to-use paste polish for furniture. Use either turpentine or white spirit,

or a mixture of both. The quantity of solvent can be varied to produce polishes of different consistencies; less solvent will make a firmer polish.

Melt the wax and slowly raise the temperature to about 70°C

(160°F). Heat the solvent to a similar temperature and then blend it with the melted wax. Carefully pour the mixture into a container, leave to cool and set, then close the container securely.

Linseed oil paste polish

250g (10oz) beeswax
500ml (1pint) linseed oil

This recipe makes a softer polish which is ideal for use on bare wood. Mix the ingredients as for the basic paste polish.

High-gloss paste polish

200g (8oz) beeswax
25g (1oz) carnauba wax
500ml (1pint) solvent

Carnauba wax, extracted from a Brazilian palm tree, is a very hard wax which has a melting point of about 85°C (185°F). It is quite expensive, but just a small amount added to the basic recipe will make a polish that is less tacky, far easier to apply, and one that will give a wonderful shine.

Cream polish

32g (1¹/₄oz) beeswax
500ml (1pint) turpentine
65ml (2¹/₂ fluid oz) pine oil
65ml (2¹/₂ fluid oz) liquid soap
250ml (¹/₂pint) soft water

Cream polish is an emulsion of wax and water – two substances which normally separate from each other. However, when the wax element (the beeswax, pine oil and turpentine) and the water element (soft water and liquid soap) are heated to the same temperature and then mixed thoroughly, a stable creamy substance is created.

Melt the wax, add the turpentine and pine oil and gently heat to a temperature of – 80°C (180°F). Mix the soap and water in another pan and heat to the same temperature. Pour the wax element into a mixing bowl, begin to stir and then slowly add the soap and water mixing continuously until a creamy consistency is achieved. Pour the polish into warmed bottles; allow to cool and then fit the caps.

Leather treatment

125g (5oz) beeswax
250ml (¹/₂pint) tallow (see page 52)
250ml (¹/₂pint) neatsfoot oil

This recipe is an excellent preparation for waterproofing shoes. It is equally effective on leather coats, upholstery and riding tack. Gently heat all the ingredients to about 70°C (160°F); blend them together and pour into containers.

Encaustic art

Encaustic art

Over two thousand years ago the ancient Greeks, Romans and Egyptians were using beeswax as a painting medium. The wax was melted in a palette over a charcoal fire which kept it warm and workable. This wax, rendered liquid by the heat, was then coloured with pigments and used to create beautiful long-lasting portraits and pictures.

Today coloured, light-fast beeswax can be melted, using modern methods, to produce spectacular and individual images. Abstracts and landscapes take on a glow with the warm wax colours. Each one is unique; it is impossible to recreate or copy it exactly. It is easy to rework paintings using heat as a solvent, and many techniques can be employed to achieve amazing results. The finished, cooled encaustic painting can be 'polished' to produce a soft, natural sheen, and unlike an oil painting , it does not need to be varnished. It will last a lifetime and longer.

Opposite
FANTASY CASTLE
I started out painting a general landscape in blues, purples and reds, and then using the stylus tool I added the castle and the long, winding footpath.

Materials and equipment

You will need a few unusual tools for this craft, but they are all readily available in craft shops or by mail order.

Wax colours

Wax colours are made from beeswax, light-fast pigments and resins. You can buy lots of different colours including gold, silver and bronze. You can also melt and mix the colours to make your own unique palette.

Do not try using commercial wax crayons; their colour content is usually too thin to be effective in encaustic art and they produce very poor results.

Painting card

Use a non-absorbent card with a smooth, shiny surface. It is available in white, black and a range of other colours. The backs of shiny old greetings cards are well worth experimenting with.

Backing paper

You will need a supply of cheap plain backing paper, larger than the painting card, to protect your working surface from hot wax. Change the paper as necessary to

1. Coloured beeswax blocks.
2. Hot-air gun (paint stripper).
3. Painting cards.
4. Polishing tissue.
5. Backing paper.
6. Scribing tools.
7. Encaustic stylus with hot brush head.
8. Encaustic stylus with heated point.
9. Low-temperature soldering iron.
10. Encaustic iron.
11. Cleaning tissue.
12. Work board.

avoid transferring unwanted colour to your painting. You can use old telephone directories as backing paper, but take care with printed paper as the hot iron may lift the print and transfer it to your painting.

Encaustic iron

The encaustic iron is used for general applications of wax . You can buy a temperature-controlled encaustic iron or you can use a small travel iron. Do not use steam irons because the holes in the sole will affect the application of wax and they will also get clogged up with use. Never leave a hot iron (or stylus tool) unattended. Always clean the iron and other tools when not in use. Never leave them switched on with wax still on them.

Encaustic stylus

The encaustic stylus has a heated point which is used for the application of finer detail. You can also use a low-temperature soldering iron. In addition, the tool can also be fitted with a hot brush head which can be shaped to achieve different effects.

Scribing tools

These pointed tools are used to scrape away applied wax to reveal fine white lines. I have a number of scribers all with different shaped points. Be inventive and try out tools which may give interesting effects.

Hot-air gun

Although not essential, a hot-air gun is a useful addition to your toolbox. Take great care when

using this tool as it gets very hot and can burn the card if you play it too long on one spot.

Tissue paper

Keep a supply of soft paper tissue beside your work board to clean the iron and other tools between colours. I use a folded up pad of toilet tissue, and simply tear off sheets when I need a clean surface.

You will also need some soft tissue to polish the finished paintings.

Work board

I use a small wooden lectern to work on. It is about 375 x 300mm (15 x 12in) and has a small block attached to the back of the top edge so that it sits on the work surface at a slight angle.

SNOWY MOORS
This simple landscape (larger than actual size) uses all the basic techniques of this medium. The snow on the tops of the mountains was applied with a hot brush head.

59

Painting a landscape

Here I show you how to paint a simple landscape, step by step, using the basic techniques.

First of all, set the iron to a low temperature – a 'nylon' setting is ideal. When the iron is at the right temperature the wax, when applied to the sole plate, will melt immediately and trickle down slowly when you stand the iron up. If the iron is too hot, the wax will begin to smoke, and painting control will be impossible. If the temperature is too cool, the wax will be sticky and the iron will not glide across the card.

Laying down the sky

For this type of sky I use the sweeping technique to achieve a smooth subtle blend of colours.

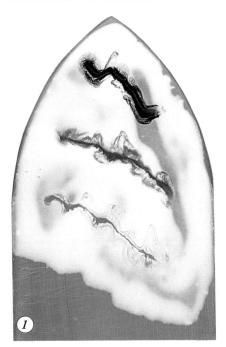

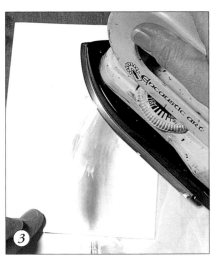

1. Apply a white wax liberally over the iron area as illustrated and then streak in a small amount of rust, yellow ochre and golden yellow in three diagonal lines.

2. Place the painting card in a portrait position on your work board. Gently sweep the iron from the top to the bottom of the card and then back up again. Cover about one half of the card with wax.

A lightness of touch is essential; too heavy a hand will simply scrape all the wax off the card.

3. Continue sweeping back and forth until the rust and yellows have blended and softened into the white. Load on more white wax and streaks of colour if you are dissatisfied with your first attempt. Any wax that goes over the edge will be absorbed by the backing paper.

When it gets dirty, change the backing paper to prevent the iron from picking up muddy colour and transferring it on to your painting.

4. You must clean the sole plate and edges of the iron between the application of different colours. Keep a pad of folded up toilet tissue on the work table, and wipe the iron on this after every painting action.

Defining the horizon

I now add distant mountains as a horizon, applying the colour via the tip and one edge of the iron.

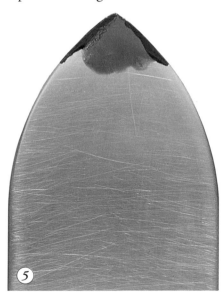

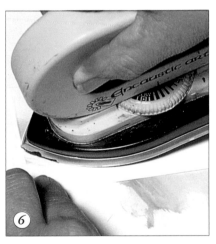

5. Load a small amount of yellow ochre on the tip of the iron. Then run a block of rust down the sides to coat both the edge and a small part of the base around the yellow ochre.

6. Turn the card to a landscape position. Starting at the left-hand side, roughly where you want your mountain range to begin, angle the iron slightly and gently run it across the card, drawing the outline of hills and mountains, using the edge furthest from you. The wax will dribble down to the working edge of the iron and on to the card.

7. Complete the mountain range in several stages, cleaning and reloading the iron with wax as necessary, until you have worked across the whole card. Do not work any area too much – you want to achieve good sharp lines.

61

Adding foothills

For the gently sloping foothills in front of the horizon I use just the flat tip of the iron to sweep some contours across the picture, working colour into the remaining unpainted area of the card.

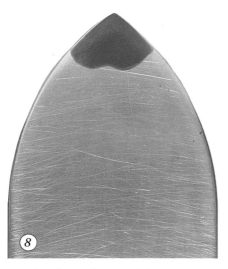

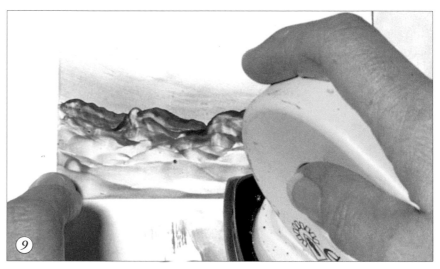

8. Load just the tip of the iron with yellow ochre.

9. Work a range of hills slightly lower down the card, in front of the background mountains. Then, using a zigzag motion, sweep the iron backwards and forwards, working down the sheet until there is a layer of wax over the whole surface. It does not matter about the look of the foreground area because this will change in subsequent stages.

Working up the foreground

I am now going to use a dabbing technique to add some life to the foreground.

10. Pick up the card and hold one of its top corners with your thumb and two fingers as illustrated. The card must be able to flex slightly as you dab it with the iron. Now, using a thoroughly clean iron, dab it on and then off the lower part of the card very quickly.

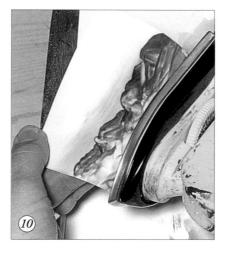

Dabbing, which creates a pattern of rivulets and veins (so much associated with this art medium) is done with the middle part of the base of the iron.

If the curved edge of the iron touches the wax already on the card you will get arc marks which will spoil the effect.

Dabbing can be done with a clean iron to give light veining to existing wax, or with more wax loaded to give heavier definition.

11. *Work across the card until you have a pleasing pattern that suggests distant foliage.*

12. *Lightly dab a block of rust colour all over the base of the iron to form a veined effect as shown.*

13. *Dab the iron on to, and then off, one of the bottom corners of the card. Move across to the other corner and dab again. Your image should now have some darker veining in these areas to simulate foreground grasses and bracken.*

Adding detail

I have now created a landscape with a sky, a horizon (the distant mountains) and some foreground images. I want to balance the picture by adding some detail that will bring it to life. This is also the opportunity to cover any blemishes that you want to hide.

You can add detail using the tip of the iron, a hot brush head or pointed stylus. If you use a clean tool (with no added colour) you can create white images by 'cutting' through the wax on the surface of the card. Alternatively you can apply extra colour and shape it with the tools to form coloured images.

> Practise the use of the encaustic tools on spare pieces of card to see the various effects that you can achieve. Try and get a feel for the right amount of wax needed, and the control necessary before you start on the picture itself.

14. First I use the tip of the iron. This makes rather broad images, which you can twist into flat-bladed grasses, etc. Load up colour by sliding the tip and a short part of one edge of the iron across a block of rust-coloured wax. Do not take up too much colour or it may drip off the tip before you want it to.

15. Starting at the base of the picture, draw in some grass just to the right of centre. Apply the tip of the iron (with the loaded edge uppermost) to the card and gently stroke upwards, with a twisting action, to form blades of grass.

16. Now I use the hot brush head. You have far more control with this than with the tip of the iron, and you can alter the shape of the brush to get different effects.

Flatten the brush head and then load it by dabbing it on to the rust-coloured block of wax. Working from the bottom of the picture, apply the brush in a gentle swirling motion to create some ferns in the middle foreground.

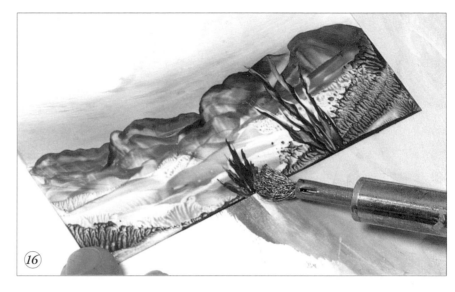

17. Simple birds can be drawn using the tip of the iron, but you get much better results using a hot pointed stylus.

Dip the tip of the stylus into the block of wax taking up a tiny spot of colour. Now make two short flicking strokes, one from the middle upwards to the right and then from the middle upwards to the left. You will then have a bird in flight.

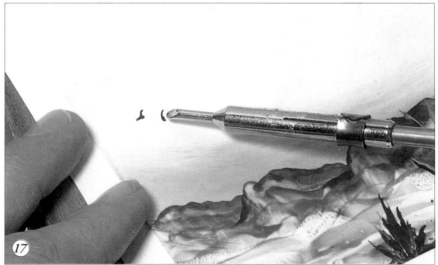

OTHER TECHNIQUES FOR ADDING DETAIL

You can also add detail using scribing tools. They are used to scrape away wax to create white areas (or the colour of the painting card) in the picture. Use them to scrape back paths or, perhaps, to clear small areas for distant lakes in a country scene. An example of this technique is shown in the 'Moorland stream' painting on page 68.

Touches of colour may also be drawn directly on to the painting with dry wax. Use a blunted corner of the wax (this will be softer on the card) and blend colours with a finger or cotton bud. (See 'Blue canyon' on page 69.)

Polishing

When you are satisfied with the finished work, leave it on one side to cool completely (this takes less than a minute). On inspection you will notice that the dry wax has a dull matt finish; now is the time to make it gleam.

18. Make a loose pad of soft paper tissue. Gently polish the picture to raise the matt appearance to a beautiful, natural shine that really brings the painting to life.

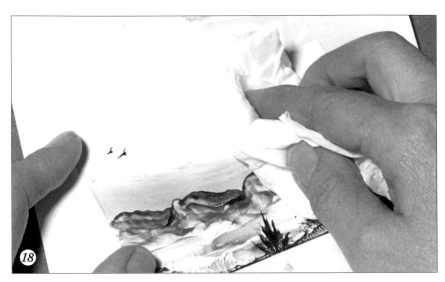

19. The finished picture. Frame it and hang it on the wall, or mount it on a folded piece of white or coloured card and make a greetings card. Small pictures are particularly suitable for this treatment.

Opposite
ARIZONA DESERT
This more advanced desert scene was painted on a larger piece of card, using the same colour range and techniques used in the demonstration picture. You can paint on even larger surfaces but, with the limited size of the iron, it can prove difficult to load sufficient wax to spread colour right across the sheet.

Encaustic art

Encaustic art

Here are just a few other ideas for encaustic landscapes. Why not experiment with the different techniques and see the wonderful effects you can create? Try monochrome pictures, or rub the sky in streaks, or have no sky at all. Or, paint a night scene in blacks and greys, a radiant sunset, or a snowy landscape with subtle blue shadows. The choice is yours.

SCOTTISH HIGHLANDS
The pine tree in the foreground was painted using the hot brush.

FOXGLOVES
All the background colour was applied with the iron, but I used a heated stylus tool for the flowers.

MOORLAND STREAM
The plant in the foreground was added using the tip of the iron. When all the background area was painted in, I scraped out the shape of the stream with the scribing tool and then rubbed in the colour with a dry wax block.

Encaustic art

CHINESE SUNRISE
I have created stylised mountains for this Chinese-style design. The chop is the sign of the Dragon, while the calligraphy translates as 'Peacefulness'.

BLUE MOUNTAINS
This 'monochrome' picture is actually painted using white and blue wax.

BLUE CANYON
In this picture I used the iron to fill in the walls of the canyon and the foreground, leaving the sky free of wax. I then rubbed in the sky with dry blocks of yellow and blue.

Fantasy pictures

You can really let your hair down with fantasy pictures. You do not have to have any artistic talent to get a pleasing result. There are no rules regarding colour, shape or form – it is for you to decide! Here I have included a few of my own fantasy paintings to show you that there is no limit to what you can do.

Try covering the whole of a piece of card with a single colour, then work back into the wax, either while it is still hot or after it has cooled. Look at the result and let your imagination go to work – you may 'see' a seascape, an animal, a cave, etc. You can then use your encaustic tools to emphasize the subject.

Another way is to work a loaded iron from top to bottom of a card in the portrait position. Go back into the wax without loading any more colour. As the iron leaves the paper at the top of the painting, try gently lifting the its lower edge away from the card to allow veins to form. Again, allow your imagination to do the rest in terms of developing the picture further. Work back into the wax, scribing or using the stylus and brush head.

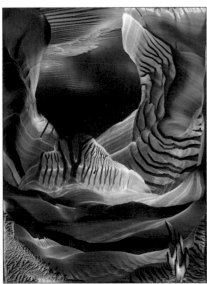

Using a hot-air gun

A hot-air gun or paint stripper can be used to create some abstract paintings, but it can also be used to good effect in some landscape pictures.

   In this abstract example, I use the hot air gun to spread and blend spots of coloured wax that have been dribbled on to a painting board. To help the blending process you must first apply a smooth layer of clear beeswax using the iron. Cover just the area on which you want to use the air gun. Allow this layer to dry.

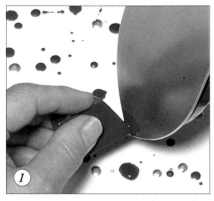

1. Hold the iron with its tip about 25mm (1in) above the clear-waxed surface of the painting card and then touch its tip with blocks of your chosen colours. Allow the melted wax to dribble randomly on to the card. If you support the painting card at an angle you will get short streaks of colour rather than round blobs.

2. Use the air gun (keeping it at least 12mm (¹/₂in) above the painting) to heat up the whole area until the wax starts to move. Tilt and turn the card and watch the effects. Do not to overwork the design. If the wax gets too hot and fugitive, switch off the gun, lay the work flat, and allow it to cool. Add more colour if you want to. Then begin to work with the gun again until you are happy with the effect.

3. The finished abstract painting in blue and silver.

Encaustic art

STORMY PEAKS
Using clear wax, gold and silver and the air gun technique on the top half of this painting produced a very dramatic sky. Mixed pastels and white will produce more subtle effects.

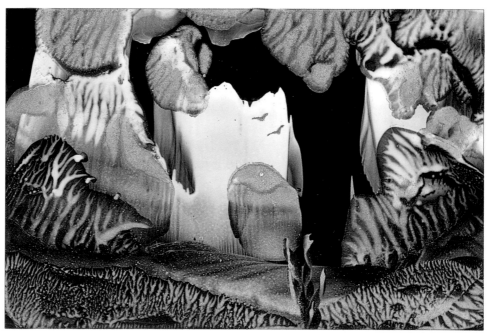

MIDNIGHT SNOW
This picture was painted using white and silver on a shiny black painting card. I used the smooth iron technique for the background areas, the dabbing technique for the mid- and foreground details, the heated stylus for the grass in the centre foreground and the hot-air gun on the large blobs of 'snow'

73

Wax crayons

Wax crayons

Making a drawing with wax crayons that you have made yourself is very satisfying. Beeswax crayons can be used successfully for sketches at home and outdoors, and for many different subjects.

The thickness of the crayons determines a broad style, and you have to look for big important shapes to give drawings strength. This is not a disadvantage; landscapes, trees, flowers and buildings can be created quickly and easily using a less detailed approach. Rubbing over objects placed under thin cartridge paper has many exciting possibilities, and you will be surprised at the interesting results you will achieve when experimenting with cotton, string, ribbon and other textured items.

Opposite
These wild flower drawings on thin cartridge paper extend the potential of beeswax crayons. Drawing a thin line on a small scale is not really possible because of the thickness of the crayons. To get the best out of them, it is better to make your flower drawings much larger than life-size, and to simplify colours and detail.

Materials

The ingredients for wax crayons can be bought at candlemakers suppliers and specialist outlets. The illustration here shows the equipment and the materials you will need:

1. *Scissors.*
2. *Masking tape.*
3. *Heat resistant jug.*
4. *Colour pigments.*
5. *Measuring spoons.*
6. *White beeswax.*
7. *China clay.*
8. *Brown paper mould.*

Recipe

1 teaspoon china clay.
1 teaspoon a colour pigment.
3 tablespoons white beeswax chips.

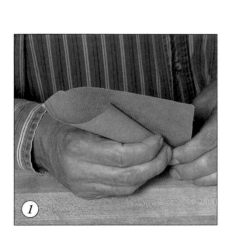

1. *Take a 150mm (6in) square of brown paper. Roll it into a cone and seal the edges firmly with masking tape.*

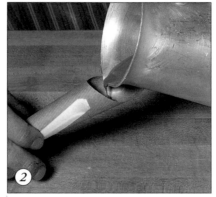

2. *Melt the wax; add the dry ingredients and then mix them thoroughly. Pour the mixture into a measuring jug and transfer the contents into the paper mould.*

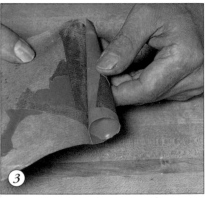

3. *Support the mould in a narrow-necked jar and allow the contents to cool. When the wax has completely set remove the paper mould. The crayon is now ready to use.*

Wax crayons

Paper

It is important to select paper that is not too rough. Cartridge paper has a slightly textured surface particularly suitable for wax crayon drawing. Ordinary writing paper is another inexpensive paper that can be used with good results.

Choosing a subject

If you have not had any experience of drawing, choose a simple subject to start with. Objects around the house and in the kitchen will give you plenty of ideas. Here I have chosen a group of apples, but you could easily draw some vegetables, or other types of fruit.

Remember that your choice of subject should be roughly the same colour as the crayons you have made. Try not to apply them too heavily because they will fill the textured surface of the paper. A light application allows the white of the paper to show through giving a unique luminosity to a drawing; this is illustrated in the sketches of wild flowers shown here. It requires only a little practice to determine the degree of pressure required.

A simple sketch of apples on thin card.

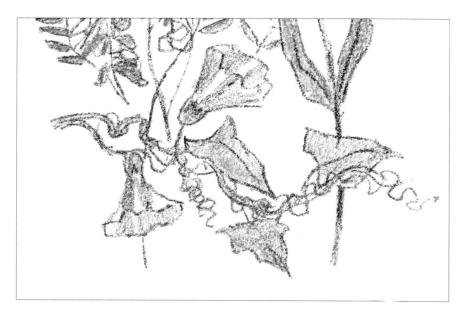

A detail of the flowers on page 74.

Wax crayons

Sketching outdoors

Beeswax crayons do not have the same richness of colour as commercially produced wax crayons, but despite this limitation they can be used successfully for sketches outdoors as well as in the home. They cannot be rubbed, or blended by smudging, which encourages a direct approach to drawing.

These two landscapes, have been drawn directly on to the surface without any preliminary roughing-in. If you do not feel confident with this method, lightly sketch in the general scheme with a pencil as a guideline.

In both pictures the main features of the landscape were drawn in with black crayon; this was also used for shadows and foreground texture. The skies were sketched in, leaving white areas to represent clouds. Certain features were picked out and filled with colour, to add depth and interest. The white of the paper was allowed to show through distant hills and fields, to add perspective to the finished drawings. The technique of overlaying colours produces further colour, as shown in the cottage door above, and the fields below.

Overlaying colours produces further colours. Here yellow was applied to the cottage door first, then blue.

Areas of blue were applied to the fields first, then yellow was worked over the top. Black crayon was used over the yellow to add shadows and texture.

Wax crayons

Scratching out

This technique involves the laying down of two colours - one on top of another; the top colour is scraped through with a craft blade to reveal the colour underneath.

Choose smooth card or paper to achieve an even covering of crayon and experiment with different colour combinations.

In the illustration below yellow wax crayon was rubbed in first, then a red overlay. The simple floral pattern was scratched out carefully with a craft blade.

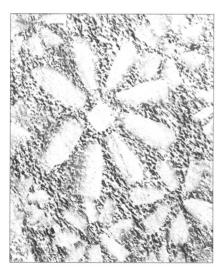

Red beeswax was applied over a yellow background and the pattern is scratched out using a craft blade.

When you are practising this technique take care not to scratch through both wax layers to the paper beneath, or the under colour will be lost.

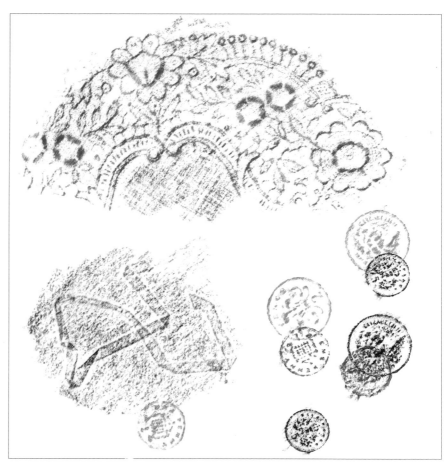

Beeswax rubbings produce some interesting effects. Here lace, folded newspaper and coins were used to create patterns and designs.

Beeswax rubbings

Rubbing over objects placed under thin cartridge paper has many possibilities. Church brass rubbing is popular, but do ask permission first if you are interested in visiting churches to try out the technique.

In the picture above objects have been selected at random. Lace can produce a lovely pattern, as shown in the impression at the top of the picture. Coins, too, can produce interesting designs. To produce overlay images rub over one coin first, then position another under the paper so that it overlaps the first image; make another rubbing.

The image on the left of the picture is beeswax rubbed over a strip cut from newspaper. First of all fold and crease the strip. Place it under the paper pressing it to make sure it is flat. Rub the wax over the raised area.

Index